What if I Told You?

What if I Told You?
Unlikely Love Poems on
Several Occasions

Michael Sharkey

Things that are far yet near. Paradise.
The course of a boat.
Relations between men and women.
Sei Shōnagon. The Pillow Book, 160. Trans.
Meredith McKinney. London: Penguin, 2006, p. 163.

Now we're all 'friends', there's no love but Like.
A.E. Stallings, Like. New York: Farrar Strauss Giroux, 2018, p. 55.

Puncher & Wattmann

First published in 2023
Published by Puncher & Wattmann
PO Box 279
Waratah NSW 2298

info@puncherandwattmann.com

NATIONAL
LIBRARY
OF AUSTRALIA

A catologue record for this book is available from The National Library of Australia.

ISBN   9781922571

Cover image by Katharina Rapp, 'The Escape Artist'
Cover design by David Musgrave

Printed by Lightning Source International

Contents

1. That you contain the world

2. What if I told you crocodiles

3. A postcard to my flatmate

4. I love you but I wonder at

5. Hand me down my public brain, Igor

6. After my inept and furtive

7. Your blue chemise

8. What do we have in common, then?

9. Knowing you were far from me

10. 'Bite me', she demanded

11. The valley where we met

12. My colleagues have suspicious minds

13. My friend, who's sipping beer

14. A drink alone in Osnabrück

15. I remember free-range sex

16. I'm fond of you. But are you

17. When conversation turns to 'My third'

18. A lie, to say my friend is sleeping

19. I should have known right from the start

20. Aunt Rose, with your Monsignor

21. And can love be one-sided

22. I wanted to sing opera

23. What sort of word is 'you'?

24. This poem, as you know

25. I've thought of you so much

26. Can love be pure

27. In comic love, a cat adores a mouse

28. O Krazy Kat and Ignatz Mouse

29. In Pogo Possum's world

30. Tony gets a glossy colour workshopped snap

31. What's the point of telling someone

32. The secretary tells us

33. The voices of two women in the train

34. A modern pillow book's list of aversions

35. My father's mother and her siblings

36. And can love poems talk of anything except themselves

37. Things that give pleasure

38. My Aunt Clare and money

39. This is just to say I got your letter

40. Do I need this? An Irish curse

41. Vivienne was brusque

42. Good morning. What a strange script

43. Why was I in the trolley Car Bar?

44. My younger daughter tells me

45. In Swanston Street

46. Forgive me, but I've fallen for the Queen of the Night

47. Two lovers are at lunch

48. What, love my neighbours as myself?

49. It had to come. The line that broke

50. My brother's business partner's the Contessa

51. Young, I was the ball boy

52. At school I read the stories of the gods

53. On the mystery planet I live on

54. Boccaccio tried and Chaucer tried

55. I'd like to think I get this business right

56. Your father was unfussed

57. The birds sing in Ukrainian

58. Love is the meaning when all's said

59. Should I ignore all other women's beauty

60. Lazaro Condo

61. A prostitute or mistress turns Madonna

62. When I get tired of being

63. Last night I thought how much I'd like to talk

64. In Tarkovsky's Solaris

65. Here I take time out to thank my family

66. John Fields, in the hospice, gives a lesson

67. They think it's sublime

68. 'What sort of love poem's that?'

69. Perhaps it happened she was tired

70. This is not a poem. You are so right.

71. My sister won 't see wattle bloom

72. The night I stayed with friends

73. No man is a hero to his dentist

74. They quoited laws that made it right

75. My parents' God

76. My parents chose to travel

77. My mother the Surrealist lived

Acknowledgments

Thanks to the editors of publications where some early drafts of poems appeared, and to Julie Chevalier, Carol Jenkins, Kevin Brophy, and David Musgrave, who variously encouraged me to be ruthless in selection.

I'm also grateful to Katharina Rapp, artist of Castlemaine, Victoria, for permission to include a detail of her painting, 'The Escape Artist', for the jacket of this publication. Katharina Rapp formally trained in Stuttgart, the Sorbonne, and La Trobe.

I dedicate this book to Kevin Ireland and Janet Wilson, along with my daughters, and the usual suspects—and especially Winifred Belmont. Con amore a ciascuno.

1

That you contain the world: the quartet
for the end of time, the seven last words,
and the Cross, the Buddha's mind,
the Prophet's head, the earth that breathes,

the sky that falls in children's tales,
the tide that ebbs, the moon's Swiss cheese,
Nijinsky's dance, Stravinsky's *Flood*—
what if I said you're all of these:

a Gadda plot, a Dowland song,
an awful mess, a Dior dress,
a Zegna suit, a pigeon shoot,

a language known inside a dream,
a Bach transcription for a lute—
not one assertion would be wrong.

2

What if I told you crocodiles ate you
in my dream and found you,
as I do, delicious? What if you are
sage and parsley, thyme and rue?

You are the lily in parched earth,
the scent of rain along the ridge,
the kapok flying in the storm,
the spotted quoll beside the dam—

each sight that penetrates the mind,
the barbed red pyracantha's bite.
What luck the world contains your flesh.

You are the garden full of birds,
the silence of the moon at night.
Could I ask more? Could I ask less?

3

A postcard to my flatmate bears a Jean-Paul Clerens image,
and I read while eating toast and drinking tea,
'My love, another little kiss from Paris for you.
Please tell Michael I will kill him if he touches you.

I'd stay another week except the weather here
is terrible and I cannot afford to rent a car.
I love mobility you know. I'm having lunch now,
onion soup, spaghetti, red wine, and smoked ham,

and scallopini, and the waitress is a treasure,
and I hope that I will do to you what these two
people on the card I'm writing on are doing.

I look forward to liaising with the countess
after staying in that monastery in Ireland. Please
tell Michael I am writing to him. Kisses. Nikola'.

Armidale 1981

4

I love you, but I wonder at your friends
whose eyes are flensing knives aimed at me.
And I wonder at my friends who knit their brows.
Why do we call these people friends?

The world will still revolve when they are ghosts.
I wonder why I love your hair dyed white.
I wonder why I love your hair dyed red.
I wear a bird of paradise on my head.

Your parents don't consider me a pest.
I love whatever's you *au naturel*. Do as you will.
You're better than the book I thought was best when I was
twelve.

The pain your body bears appals me most.
Believe me I would die to spare you that.
Sometimes I could. There have been times I thought I should.

Armidale 1979

5

Hand me down my public brain, Igor, I'm off to the office.
How many times did I feel like that, at six a.m.,
the first espresso downed, and stepping out
where the street lamps glowed in their misty haloes

on the frost-bit nature strips? In an atmosphere as dour
as a nineteen sixties masthead in the *Peking News*: 'Mao
Tsetung Thought Guides Us in Conquering Nature'.
Times I asked myself how I could justify humanities

in the academic Cold War nineteen-eighties, when to teach
was to be mocked by the mental managers bent
on altering reality, their mantras just as chilling

as Himself's 'Grasp revolution and promote production'.
Willing tools spoke gibberish, 'Teach smarter and accomplish
more with less', till pleasure gave up on the text.

New England 2009

6

After my inept and furtive fumbles,
drunken couplings, gaga discourse,
and denouements half-inched from comic opera,
to the tune of pity, scandal, and embarrassment of friends,

what sheer relief and what enlightenment
to jettison extended adolescence,
and put cliché in its box, find other language
to converse through days with you and nights in bed.

Do lovers hope the qualities they posit in another
can be picked up by osmosis? Is desire
simply struggle to annex what one admires in the other?

That's romance, the twin-soul jazz,
that some call love—discordant passion, wacky chemicals,
or custom, power politics or chance.

7

Your blue chemise. Your coloured squares.
Your copper hair. Your golden rings.
Your tennis balls. Your panama.
Your cat Rachmaninoff. Your Bach.

Your coffee mug. Your gin-and-it.
Your broken arm. Your magpie twins.
Your sunscreen cream. Your hockey stick.
Your toast and Vegemite. Your car.

Your pencil box. Your pale blue jeans.
Your magazines. Your champagne flute.
Your patchwork quilt. Your bearskin hat.

Your rowing boat. Your river rat.
Your spanakopita. Your shoes.
Your Mont Blanc pen. Your autograph.

8

What do we have in common, then?
Is this an inquisition? Roman comedy?
Are you my mother, father, or my sibling?
Anything on earth is possible now science and the law are up for
sale.

Do you like Lovecraft? Nor do I. And those
who claim to govern us—kabuki theatre?
O, agreed. Do you like scandal?
Why does Kafka seem so funny?

Now I think we're getting somewhere.
This could go on for some time:
yes, reinvention of the negative.

Tequila? No, me neither. Pass. If anybody asks,
let's say we're both confined to quarters
till we work out what we like.

9

Knowing you were far from me,
your friend arrived at midnight:
'I've been locked out. Can I stay here?'
Old line, good one. Try it sometime.

'Yes, of course, and there's your bed'.
'I've got to talk'—'No, that you mustn't…'
But of course that wouldn't answer—
I must listen to the saga of the threats,

misunderstandings, infidelities, and fights—
while torpor swept in like the sea.
I'm not Canute. It's scissors, paper,

and the rest. It was no dream. I lay broad waking.
So at last, I—need I tell you
how a mouth can stop a mouth?

10

'Bite me', she demanded. And I wouldn't,
so she bit me on my lip until it bled.
We're cysts inside each other's life, she tells me
when she comes again at midnight in her fur coat,

nothing else, imperious, 'Go out and pay the driver'.
I went out, and told him, 'Look, whatever
she paid, I'll pay double next time, take her
anywhere, some gorge, and tell her I've left the town for good'.

He grinned, 'Nice try, good luck. You people
are pure gold. How can I lose?' He left.
So thanks. I wonder where she gets the nerve,

and what I'll say to my love when she comes,
concerning bites, the alien perfume
and the tang of burning fur.

11

The valley where we met
when I returned was full of cloud.
A river flood had torn the bridge up.
Wet grass brushed bare feet.

Red-bellied black snakes paused and like the first time, went.
The house, of weathered wood, was void.
The wind and rain had warped the doors.
A window wavered in faint breeze.

Mountains ringed the valley.
Closer mist banks washed the paddocks
gone to gorse, and feral orchard.

Fruit hung leathery on branches.
In the garden where we'd sat
no moving thing was.

Bellinger River 1978

12

My colleagues have suspicious minds, Darelle,
you know the office doors stay open when a student calls.
You sashay in like Isis with a joint. Is this a tryst?
My lucky day? We kill the spliff and screw like stoats?

I say, let's not, and say we did. Who's got the energy for tricks?
I say, just write the damned assignment, hand it in.
You've got the wit. Who cares? The Hellfire Club's your shtick.
You've got the tone, like Aphrodite with an axe.

Yeah, you look good enough to eat.
Some women on this campus say your eyes are epitaphs
for guys who've left them with the kids because of you. Poor
saps.

No need to start that here. Let's skip the game.
Nice skin, for sure. But leave me mine.
C'est tout. Bonjour. Now shut the door.

Armidale 1978

13

My friend, who's sipping beer and watching beach girls
from the harbour bar announces, 'Voyeurism's all I've got,
now I am old'. Aloud, he wonders, marinaded in his past,
if a new love coming in will mean farewell to those
departing.

But passion doesn't leave so long as bodies can draw breath.
It's oxygen to teenagers on heat—and older folk.
The way our hormones screw us is a joke.
Whenever fire dies, there is still smoke.

My friend's still friendly with his former wife
though states and countries separate them now.
My case runs parallel: I don't like strife.

Some loves proceed from kindness straight to hate
when partners see life through each other's eyes:
if X was happy and Y not, apology's too late.

Port Macquarie 1981

14

A drink alone in Osnabrück where everyone has vanished
who was with me here last night—Tobias, Brigitte,
and the Africans, New Zealanders, West Indians,
Canadians—and how come that professor

from Toronto knows just where to disappear to
with that lovely woman who was waiting for him?
Now the meetings are all over,
and I pause with pen in hand, and thinking

of the pleasure of the letters I am writing
when they come to earth in houses
of my friends in other places—

and of faces, in the theatre of my mind,
yours, most of all—as people amble in
for coffee, late, and gossip. Yours sincerely.

1998

15

I remember free-range sex. It seemed like a nervous tic.
My students tell me they still pine
for the wedding bling. In time they'll learn
why Dido died. Aeneas was a prick.

Could be Robert Graves was right: man does, and woman is,
but I doubt Dido would have certified that line of his.
Her first man was her uncle, Acerbas, Herakles' priest,
and when he died, she moved to grab the treasury and flit.

Virgil claims she fell for a drifter next and died of grief.
Some die for love, and some exist for whom a partner's death
is like the dawn of freedom or a zombie's first-drawn breath.

Love is strange though times and actors change.
An embalmed cat's memorial verse in Petrarch's house proclaims,
'Laura was his second love. I was his greatest flame.'

16

I'm fond of you. But are you fond of me?
Fond's a word for crazy in the sixteenth century.
So fond am I of you I must be frail. Most would agree.
Would you say that our minds and bodies fit conformably?

I'd die for you, but please don't have a requiem sung for me.
I don't admire soppy modern hymns. Let's have some dignity.
Look! The nimbostratus clouds are buffing up their nails.
The weather persons told us there'd be hail.

And here it is. How were you born?
Oh, spare the details, please. I mean,
how did the universe conspire to make you?

Nice work, o world.
Grammar smartens up when I'm with you,
and forces time to this event with you.

17

When conversation turns to 'My third husband...', or
'As one of my ex-wives said...', I'm undecided
whether lack of will or chance made me a line-judge
when I could have been a champion in the sport of matrimony.

I'd be knocked out in the heats.
I share the Jewish joke's insistence
that insanity is doing something time and time again,
anticipating different outcomes every time—

the one-night stands, like metro trains that hesitate in loops,
or the revolving-door divorces of celebrities,
or fake adherence to political or other faith or none,

the prêt-à-porter roles we try on till identity dissolves—
we act like farmers using pesticides
and wondering why the bees refuse to live.

18

A lie, to say my friend is sleeping
underneath the earth. He's compost, now,
he's one with earth. He would have cracked jokes,
taking short-cuts with me through the General Cemetery.

'My eyes aren't good, but I love all I see',
my friend would say of such bone gardens, and 'Italians
have the right idea, to decorate their tombs with happy snaps
of those they miss'. He would have said,

'I don't believe these slogans, "In safe keeping",
"Gone aloft", "At last in peace"'
No, he who lent my fiancée the cash

to buy the dark green leather jacket she wore
on her motorbike is dead. I think of him at times—
preux chevalier et sans pareil.

i.m. KW. Wellington NZ.

19

I should have known right from the start
when we left for our honeymoon further south
with your younger sister as chaperone,
though what in God's name did she think we'd do

on the all-day train through the chill moraine
where volcanos smoked at the cusp of the plain,
or where we paused on windswept platforms where we ate the deadly
                                                        sandwiches
and drank the dark stewed tea and then the city I'd never seen

where the widdershins wind that tore through clothes
and the streets where cardigans were in vogue
and the budget hotel where at last we lodged

and your sister vanished, snug in a room elsewhere,
while our goddam window hung on a single hinge before it fell
four floors to the pavement to complete our treacle moon.

                                        1970

20

Aunt Rose, with your Monsignor
straight from a book by Morris West,
did you suppose nobody knew?
Were our senses shut?

My wife and I on a honeymoon,
guests in your bijou bach on a beach
you kept remote from city eyes,
where you could star in a private movie.

You and he inhaled martinis, as if posed
for a photo shoot for *Vogue* and *Oggi*,
strapless you, swim-shorted he,

with your air of a countess, his of a prince.
You offered midday lunch and a boat,
and your urbane style to our curious eyes.

21

And can love be one-sided, or is that another state,
say, monomania? Wizard stuff. Can one surrender
to abstraction, say like those we claim have died
for love of country? Could a country ask for more?

Can one love God? Does God enjoy, or use us?
In an Aztec codex it is written that their Lord rolls us
like marbles in his hand and laughs at us.
Dante kicked the ball of love along, adoring beauty—

and got no word in return. As if a dart could be retracted.
Provence polished pining to an art: a glance,
a blow, and life gone numb but never dumb:

the poets reaching for ambrosia and finding love
as likely as a shadow from no flesh,
or a hangman's smile, a drop of lemonade in hell.

22

I wanted to sing opera, but the notes
were always better in so many others' throats.
I bought an old guitar to learn to play
and practised till my fingers hurt each day.

I turned to pianoforte, and I tried.
My aunts and uncles laughed until they cried.
I borrowed a bass saxophone and blew
until the neighbour's Doberman howled too.

My cousin played French horn and told me, 'Well,
if anybody asks, you play like hell'.
I then picked up a violin and found

a cat on heat emitted the same sound.
I wanted to play flute and clarinet.
The world does not seem ready for the music in me yet.

23

What sort of word is 'you'? This thing called you
that's in my life—that's not you reified. The word
cannot suggest, as old songs say, the things you are....
What sort of dictionary or library would you be?

What sort of nation or what polity? What country
and what history and what skies? What tribes?
What music? The bandura? Would I know your epic songs?
I am a stranger to your shores.

What language should I choose? What notes and coins
are current there? What streets and plazas, lanes and cafés
and apartments? Who lives high up on the hills?

Will there be snow? What covered stalls and open markets!
Shall we breakfast at the hotel with the people we see
upside-down reflected in the lake? Let's eat the world!

24

This poem, as you know,
is not about you or itself:
it is itself and nothing else,
as you are you, as trees are trees,

as rock is rock, and not about the trees or rock.
No metaphor can cross that space,
not even 'is itself, as you are you,
as rock is rock, as trees are trees.'

So you and I remain discrete,
though trees and rock
and you and I make an event

inside a poem, where words flicker
like a thought in meditation,
hold their sway a moment, go.

Armidale 1982

25

I've thought of you so much you don't exist.
What is it like to hold you in my mind?
The painted eyes on portraits seem to fix
on something far beyond the gazers' stare.

Could any of these ghosts abolish you,
who are the shadow of a shadow in my mind?
In all its walls of icons, which is you?
What language would a simulacrum speak?

A gush of cafe-conversations starts,
the phone-chat voices that insist that what is speaking
still exists, an urgent murmuring

that's far too indistinct, like mind's attempts to touch
the shadow of a shadow, conjure memory
of a morning in the evening. None will do.

Armidale 1982

26

Can love be pure when what we love is wrapped
inside a body, meat that's parcelled into skin?
Are we salamis, mystery bags, decay included,
past all cure, planned obsolescence

by intelligent design? Where's love in that?
No answer comes. Is silence peace?
The mind has other work to do, like grass
when bees and butterflies go where such workers go?

How can it be love outlives what was loved
before what made it living ceased?
To be bereft of that, can that be life?

Old painters knew to leave a fly or bug about to die,
the *nature morte*, that seems alive and yet is not,
deceiving shadow that held breath, the hide of life that teases us.

27

In comic love, a cat adores a mouse
and is in turn loved by a cop who is a dog
spelt K-O-P. What world is this, friends, as
John Berryman, the funniest of poets,

might have said. Or was it Herriman who saw
the world as people loving hopelessly but never
giving up? Their love made sense—when all
the business of America was business

that would fail and when pursuit of pleasure,
which would also go west, seemed what all
created equal persons, but who were not, made their goal—

Jay Gatsby's world of haves and have-nots, careless drivers,
and a dream that sanctioned crime for passion's sake.
Love, let's be comics speaking truth.

28

O Krazy Kat and Ignatz Mouse, philosophers
of the sublime, you recognised that language is the way
that we misunderstand each other. Long before
your static panels showed us shapes and scenes that shifted,

Aristotle and the sceptics answered Plato
and his hit-squad with the news that language is
how we may find things far more slippery though
as real as bricks a mouse could bean a cat with—

Kat who comes back every time, misreading
brickbat for bouquet—as we, who slipped
into the panels of life's comedy while getting on

with what we'd thought the business
of our lives, discovered love that rained down
on us like an ideal ton of bricks.

29

In Pogo Possum's world, a worm's a little tad
assuring passers-by it isn't bait; cross-talking bats
in checkered pants and derby hats play cards
and make Beckettian cracks, exchanging names

filched from *Pal Joey*: 'I'm Bewitched', 'I am Bewildered',
'I am Bothered'—just like Yeats's 'Hic' and 'Ille'.
'Who am I?' games—while an alligator smokes
a blunt cigar. A wily fox and bearcat think of ways

to eat a guest; a selfish owl relieves his host
of his last sandwich, and a beaver's out of sorts
to find her wedding to a pigeon is called off.

Against all odds, Churchy La Femme's a turtle, in a cloak
and pirate hat proclaiming Dada; while a bashful
possum serenades unlikely love, as I do, mon amour.

Tony gets a glossy colour workshopped snap of Cher
in all her plumage, signed, 'For Tony, happy birthday, kisses,
Cher'. His teenage sons have got him twigged.
He says, 'I'll frame that snap.' He wonders if she gets

a lot of poems, says he'd better write a tribute.
'Great', I say, 'You can't do worse than all the doggerel
of adoring fans online'. I think about that later,
can't recall a single poem to a singer that ain't schmalz.

And never mind the dedications. Where do poets get the notion
Cher, Beyoncé, Britney Spears, Shakira, Kylie, Alizée,
Madonna, Taylor Swift, and Lorde knows who, have time

to ransack small-press chapbooks in the chance
that they'll discover (sing it louder) they've played Muse
to the poet laureate of Mother of Ducks Lagoon?

What's the point of telling someone, when you're young,
'I'd like to age with you'? Get hip, Li Po.
Skin will turn to mottled cloth, and teeth long to be free,
and when the glory has departed from your own and every

ancient lover's head, and tufts as big as mice have sprung
from ears and nostrils, thickets grown where eyebrows clung,
don't tell me you'll still be besotted. You will sport
more comic threads and ugly shoes than you wear now.

Pull down, I say, your beehive hair, but shave your head?
A tattooed freakshow, you'll grow weirder every day.
And where will sweet exhilaration after sex be? Now, you lick

each other's sweat and juice from breasts and throats
and tender parts, but life will seem a Chinese curse
when zippers mean a gurney, or a bypass of the heart.

32

The secretary tells us in the common room, 'He whistled,
and he sang all round the house.
He liked to watch the women's tennis.
He made noises when he ate.

He couldn't cook.
He said he'd leave it up to me.
As if it's hard.
He hated squash and sweet potato.

And he liked it when our daughter's daughters brushed and
combed his hair.
"There is a time and place", I said,
"I'd like to travel". He said, "Go. I'll be all right". And so I did.

My friend and I went to Japan. We took our time.
Afterwards, his sisters asked if life with him was easy.
Well, he couldn't help himself. What could I say?'

Armidale 1978

33

The voices of two women in the train up to the highlands
rise in volume and insistence as we leave the coastal plain.
The younger: 'Mother, they're not Germans. I said, gerberas,
they're growing round the farm. Just wait,

you'll see them from the window of the lovely room
we've set up for your stay. A field of gerberas in full bloom'.
'And are the Germans all in uniforms, then, dear?'
'No, Mum, they're flowers. Flowers don't wear any clothes.

They're blossoms. They're named after someone German'.
'Dear, I don't want naked Germans coming in the bedroom window.
Alec fought them, as you know. He didn't like them'.

'No, Mum, flowers. They're not Germans. Mum, just listen,
we've got gerberas growing all around the house'.
'So why do Germans want to come in bringing flowers?'

34

A modern pillow book's list of aversions:
bores who answer, 'How are you?' in minute detail;
shouts and whining in the next-door flat: the tourists have arrived;
a politician who mouths slogans that would make a dybbuk gag;

appalling movies hailed as art;
all baby photos sent as evidence the parents have gone daft;
a guest who says, 'I'll stop in passing' and remains till midnight's
passed;
a mogul businessman who brags he pays no tax;

Jack Kerouac's, and all his scaly mates' remarks on women;
every shock-jock—when a stranger talking filth invades my house,
should I be glad or call the police to take the ugly thing away?

And letters that we write asserting lies as truth
to relatives and friends, at births and marriages and deaths,
and those to lovers when love's dead.

35

My father's mother and her siblings slaked their thirst
for melodrama sparring with their partners.
Their imagination fed on shilling shockers, gossip columns,
police reports, and silent movies. Heavy breathing was

what possums did in ceilings and what heaving bosoms wrung
from half-dressed floozies and their hunks on stage or screen.
Their men were sullen, keeping nit in backyard sheds
with bugs and spiders, rats and mice. The way one does.

No handsome prince or princess sprang from Mills and Boon
confections or from Hollywood romances to accost them in the flesh.
The B-grade market fed them pap and glitz.

My sad ancestors signed up out of duty to the pulps,
and went to war, and met more horrors
than they ever saw in print or at the flicks.

36

And can love poems talk of anything except themselves?
Can this? I doubt it. So I never made a novel of my life.
De Sade said, 'Nature granted me these urges.
To resist them would have been to outrage nature'.

We were not Bernard de St Pierre's unknowing innocents
at large in a naughty world to find our way.
It was our coming into being that amazed us.
We exulted in discovery of each other, in our fate.

Not for us the nihilist's desire to destroy what's in the mirror.
It was infancy again—as when I walked
around the margin of a broad lake with my cousin,

one of dozens, in my family that holds multitudes—
we passed from sight of parents, aunts and other social clutter.
We were young, and green, and awestruck, for that matter.

37

Things that give pleasure:
truckers' names for trucks: The Octopussy,
Jumper Thumper, Hopper Stopper, Kanga Banger,
Such is Life, and Agro's Beast. The bracing honesty!

At Sydney University, the gargoyles on the Quadrangle
are based on actual people.
I have met them on the ground
in many places I have worked in.

Third, I like the way a sports coach claims the opposition
didn't help his team to play their normal game.
It sounds a whole lot better than 'We lost'.

Another thing I like about some names that rise in memory
is so many of their owners once said, smiling at me,
'So, still writing poetry, are you?' And they are dead.

38

My aunt Clare and money. Cash and Carry. Hide and seek.
The plain and purl. The smoke and fire. Tooth and nail.
The lawn and sprinkler. Whip and spur. The horse and cart.
The cheese and pickle. Pie and mash. The egg and bacon.

Night and day. The Pope and Bovril. Heads and tails.
The bread and butter. Red and black. The cat and mouse.
The Ace and Jack. The steak and chips. The horse and rider.
Dust and ashes. Now you see it now you don't.

Her oldest sister falling ill, Clare thrashed the car
to see her, pick her up and take her home,
and told her sister, 'No one seems to want to see you.

Change your will'. Her sister did, and at her funeral,
Clare declared (I guess the pun is on the nail),
'I'll never be poor anymore'. But then she died.

39

This is just to say I got your letter saying,
'Give me back my heart, you desert rat'.
I laughed so hard I nearly cried.
You write side-splitting farewell notes.

I hope you'll make a book one day.
You have the gift, so many gifts, e.g.,
the music and the books that I've recovered
from the op-shops where you left them,

each still with its dedication, 'Jennie, all my love,
from Michael'. That was low. How many people have
the *Sergeant Pepper's Lonely Hearts Club* album,

signed by each of the Fab Four? I hand it to you.
You and I looked good together, for a time
were good together. Did you have to scratch the tracks?

Darlinghurst 1966

40

Do I need this? An Irish curse, an evil eye
and a packet of prawn heads wrapped up
in *The Sun* came home to roost.
The albatross around my neck had twins,

and the world I knew was a carnival trick;
the penny dropped, the balloon went up.
All ordinaries collapsed. A military band
with your name on a flag marched in

through a hole in my head.
Heart in déshabillé, mind in a sling,
and horoscope stuck on hold,

I discovered life wasn't fun for a zombie.
How else explain how it is to be caught
in the rabbit trap called love?

Armidale 1979

41

Vivienne was brusque to point of rudeness.
'You get into bed', she said. And sometime later,
'If my father saw us doing this, he'd kill you.
He's a policeman. A Commissioner, in fact'.

My heart leapt up. I asked her, 'Does he do that
to your lovers?' She inspected me as if I'd
sprouted leaves, then as if talking to herself, said,
'Now you've spoiled it'. I was banjaxed.

So I never wrote a poem on the trees I saw that year
outside my window on the street above the harbour,
nor her father, whom I never met, although it seems

I owe him for the lesson that his lovely daughter taught.
She dressed and put her distance glasses on, and said,
'Don't try to get up, I'll remember you like this'.

Potts Point, 1965

42

Good morning. What a strange script.
You were wondering all week? I wondered too.
You're right. We fit each other well.
Let's say the urgency of flesh, hard to ignore and to forget.

What is this then? Infatuation? No, me neither.
That's bad grammar. Goes to show. A cigarette?
We haven't met in bed before. We should write songs.
You hardly slept? I didn't, too. He's mad for you, your man—

I almost said last night, 'Come in'.
I pitied him. You're beautiful and cruel.
I heard him two floors down there, calling out at every door,

and all the girls replying, 'Sweetie, just have patience, wait your turn'.
And then the boyfriend of the timpanist upstairs, with 'O my word, no,
no girls here!' We shouldn't laugh. Where were we, then?

Kings Cross 1967

43

Why was I in the Trolley Car Bar? Piqued.
And you? Don't say it was the music. So we clicked.
The way you do. The trouble is, there isn't much to say
the morning after. 'Who are you?' shows no respect,

and 'What do you do for a crust?' is peasant talk, and
'Was it good for you?' distressing past contempt.
Some joker with a warped mind called this room the 'Bridal
                                                    Suite'.
Perhaps a midget with insomnia in love with busy streets?

I used to like the Cross at dawn. You too?
That radio next door can't drown the Japanese pearl traders'
                                            party's snores.
That was some binge they had last night. Shall we explore

what they call breakfast? Good-bye, then. It was a treat
to meet you too. I'd send a morning-after poem
though we're incognito, and the sky's Heidsieck on ice.

                                    Kings Cross 1968

44

My younger daughter tells me I am shallow.
I am in the sere and yellow, but I'm see-through,
as my mother used to say. My daughter's angry on the phone.
She says, 'You're not a proper parent or grandparent.

You won't own your own emotions'. I'm a sucker for such lines.
The price of being older is to take the flak of youth.
I am backdated. That's the truth. Or never grew up, so I'm told.
I say, 'Millennia back when you were young and I was not

a walking cash machine, you wouldn't speak to me like this'.
She tells me to attempt the anatomically impossible.
Her voice could drown a coffee grinder when it's smashing beans.

I question my morality that causes such distress,
add, 'I'm a puddle framing sky, all mud beneath.
I call it grief'. She says, 'No, you're beyond belief'.

45

In Swanston Street,
the twenty-somethings
dress like manga fantasies.
Heads turn, and mouths say, Wow!

These lovely shoppers from Japan have turned themselves
to mobile ciphers, like the logos
on the glossy bags they carry,
like their perfect hair and makeup:

they are walking dollar bills,
the proof that money can buy candy for the eye if not the mind.
They'd make Karl Marx and Friedrich Engels want to die,

they are responses to the call to free up drugs.
They are the neoliberals' wet dream.
They devour Milton Friedman and the world.

Forgive me, but I've fallen for the Queen of the Night
once more, in the lovely theatre in Lviv.
I knew you'd understand. I was in tears
as fear and pity did the rounds, and when

the flute produced a bestiary on stage,
I held my breath. By rights, I should have been ashamed
to see the fight of justice, cast as female,
and enlightenment as male. I wondered

which was the greater tyrant then—Sarastro, quick
to punish those who do his work,
or the nameless Queen whose detestation drives the plot.

When she commands her daughter, 'Kill Sarastro',
I recalled that Sigmund Freud believed the opera's plot insane.
What did he want? A Mills and Boon with happy tunes?

47

Two lovers are at lunch on one another in the doorway of the Girls Bar
at the Royal George Hotel. I think, Keep at it, kids. There'll be a time when
it will be 'Christ, if my love were in my arms and in my bed again'.
And one is Janice, dressed in denim, at the entrance who calls out to me,

'Come in'. The bouncer eyes me, and when Janice says, 'It's okay,
she's a girl', the heavy checks me out again and says,
'I've seen some ugly women in my time, but you're the ugliest
I've seen in twenty years'. He lets me in. I say, 'Thanks, handsome'.

And then, 'Janice, when did you give up on Jim?'
'I never had much luck with men', she says, 'so I just let the best me win.
It seems to work out now. And you?' 'So-so', I say,

'You had me lassoed way back when'. 'And now?' We laugh.
'You're good?' she asks. I say, 'Best I can be',
and toast, 'To women', kiss, and leave her with her friends.

                                        Forest Lodge 1968

What, love my neighbours as myself? And when they love
with cutlery and insults aimed at walls and at each other
and through windows and the door that slams and opens,
lock being busted, while they smash up chairs and fittings,

in the flat below, until their kitchen's filled with sobs
and crockery shards and silence but for weeping
in their desperate grief and coupling? Later, John and Tui
with their 'You know how it is' looks, to my front door, asking

'Could you lend a plate, some glasses and some forks?'
until my kitchen is depleted with this ritual. Then the soapie
once again, at first contrite, and then crescendo—

'Lousy rat, I know your style, I smell her perfume on your clothes',
and he, 'You blame me?' This is like Ravel's *Bolero*
where no theme can be developed but obsession, call it love.

Cremorne NSW 1972

49

It had to come. The line that broke the audience up
when the visiting poet spoke about his lover's breasts
as plastic bags of honey, then continued, dead-set earnest,
lifting lines from ancient sutras and the Song of Songs

in praise of his current squeeze's fertile crescent.
It was Petrarch's 'I'll have blason with the lot'. Just when
we thought that some male poet could attempt erotic verse without
appearing as a Klexter of the patriarchal Klavern,

here he was, attempting nuance, calling spade a bloody shovel.
Do all heterosexual poets have tin ears? Do gay male poets?
I've heard some declare their lover's balls are pigskin bags

of marbles, and how spit makes fucking easy.
I've heard women laugh at such lines, saying, 'True, how
very true'. My ears resound with a Zildjian hiss.

Armidale 1981

50

My brother's business partner's the Contessa,
and his only foreign tongue the one she slips between his lips.
She deals in luxury, smart clothes and leather goods.
He deals in putting things together: parts from China,

Vietnam, the Czech Republic, anywhere at all to keep the wolf
at bay: insect repellents that make summer living easy,
merchant banking, poaching seafood, selling crabs to city restaurants,
and buying rural property to flick on to the greenhorns,

moving in and renovating slums and moving on, and debt collecting,
and acquiring modern art and wines to hoard and auction off.
And world travel, always first class, cars to dream of, working lunches,

and the mistresses he's set up: do I envy? One side
of our ancestry consists of gold prospectors: chancers,
who made good, as he has done. And me? I write.

51

Young, I was the ball boy every Saturday at tennis until one
when I played C-grade, moving up to level B.
My pro-grade father was relentless
in his coaching, and his mantra, 'Watch the ball'.

I gathered tennis balls in buckets, took them to him
where he stood close to the net to bat them back to kids in turn.
A well-stacked girl with the air of Brigitte Bardot
put me off my stroke each week. So did her boyfriend,

who sat growling on the sideline while I played mixed
doubles with her. On the centre court, her friend,
a Botticellian beauty, tall and svelte and blonde

as Vitti in *L'Eclisse*, was paired in matches
with my dad. They were so splendid
we all watched and held our breath.

2022

52

At school I read the stories of the gods
in Virgil, Ovid, and the texts that were taboo.
Of course, I knew the tales were cod,
but I was captivated by the scams those shysters used

to con each other into sex. Molesters
with eternity to spare, and more grotesque
than debonair, those models of deception
never seemed to give a rat's for contraception.

More than this, I think, they had a yen for mortal things,
like bathing in cool streams on summer days,
or wolfing down a plate of figs and honey cakes.

They envied humans' pleasure in a lunch of bread and cheese
and missed the savour of new wine, and most of all,
when work was done, the simple luxury of sleep.

53

On the mystery planet I live on, I take a tram.
'L'amour est un oiseau rebelle, que nul ne peut apprivoiser',
two girls sing softly at the back. A man
with decorated skin bawls out, 'Speak English, bitches',

and an older woman sitting next to him joins in,
'Yeah, piss off back to where you came from'. Fellow travellers
turn to phones or feet, and conversation dies.
Whatever goes on in the painted man's brain,

life goes on outside his skin. I am no hero,
but I say, 'The song's from opera, it's about
the way love goes'. The creep rebounds, 'Are you

their friend? Where are you from?' I say, 'A place
where people hesitate to threaten those who can't retaliate,
and think of love instead of hate'.

Melbourne 2014

54

Boccaccio tried and Chaucer tried, and Tasso tried
and Shakespeare tried, to guess how women thought
and what they wanted. Enheduanna, Sappho,
and the poets named Sulpicia could have told them,

Lady Ise, and Marie de France, and nuns who wrote
from convent cells in Asia and in Europe could have told them.
Madeleine de l'Aubespine, Vittoria Colonna,
and Ann Bradstreet, and the women Doctor Johnson chose

to leave out of his *Lives of the English Poets* could have told them.
Emily Bronte and Elizabeth Barrett Browning and
Christina G. Rossetti, Emily Dickinson and even Lady Gaga

could have told them, while the men kept tossing off
ideas about what women wanted. And the wonder is the women
had the patience to write time and time again as if for children.

55

I'd like to think I get this business right
without the props—the hearts that beat like Onan
pumps, the compass legs that grow erect,
the bodies blazoned like a feast, the prêt-

à-porter sighs and groans to some svelte idol
looking like a Sacher-Masoch prototype
of sex in furs, cool dominatrix who could show
an Aztec priest what heartless means.

I don't require puppy fat kids' heads
with budgie wings, or a fresh-shucked woman standing naked
on a half-shell while her dopey son shoots darts

at beefcake rent-boys playing coy.
The mise-en-scène's all wrong for us.
I don't like camp. You don't like fuss.

56

Your father was unfussed about his mastery of Zen.
The nineteen-sixties were stuffed full of it. The seventies retailed it,
made a beauty contest of it: 'I can sit for seven hours';
'Why, that's nothing, I can sit entire days without an ache'.

I wondered at my bhikku friends who quoted Kerouac
and fretted that a tea-bowl was too smart, a sleeping mat too
                                        comfortable,
a saffron robe too bright. A few declared the toilet was feng shui,
the tamari sauce delicious, and that weevils in the rice were Buddhists too.

Some years ago, your family asked your father, 'Can we go and see
the ocean?' He said yes, and drove you there, and without pausing
on a headland said, 'The ocean. Now you've seen it'. Then drove home.

I thought of this when I read Suzuki Roshi said he'd like to see the
                                        cherry
blossoms in a distant garden, and a student drove him there, and Roshi
said, 'That's very beautiful', as flowers came in view, 'Now let's go back'.

57

The birds sing in Ukrainian,
the Polish buses' drivers sip on pop.
A concrete angel sweats in mist.
Old tourists fuss with walking frames and sticks.

A guide explains the graveyard is a book.
Some listeners check their mobile phones, take pics.
Effigies of mourning women lean on family tombs.
A marble group's alight in filtered sun.

Flesh is not the only thing that's wearing badly here.
Julian Markowski's sleeping woman wears dark stains.
The past grows meaning in accord with what we do.

Some people walking here will meet with siblings, parents,
loves. I think of my own forbears, gone from view
in formal suits and Empire gowns and silhouettes.

Lviv 2013

58

Love is the meaning when all's said and done.
And words are the meaning, 'All shall be well',
for example, wraps the wounded and the missing,
all who sleep rough with the sky their only roof.

In time of peace, in time of war, the tongues of bells
are eloquent, reminding those who wait in queues
for visas they should give up all hope here.
The poor in spirit always will be far from well.

The age we live in makes it seem that nothing
good can come out of it. And while we wait,
the animals are leaving, from the smallest to the largest.

We shrug, say that this is life.
Our love is blasphemy where we refuse to grant it
to the least of every organism keeping us alive.

2021

Should I ignore all other women's beauty,
apparitions that have stopped me in my tracks?
The waiter in an Osnabrück café, who turned the heads of men and women
who laid down their phones and cups and ceased to speak.

Another time—so sudden that I paused to gaze in awe—
a woman reading in a café in an Aachen autumn dawn beside the Dom.
And Melbourne, in a plane departure lounge,
a woman came, and all eyes turned, and all talk ceased.

What does it mean? I never died and went to heaven.
I am transfixed here on earth that holds such wonders.
It's as if a butterfly broke into song.

These visions of such beauty have exalted me—as much
as prayers of monks are said to please God, and by doing so gain grace.
I wish my poems might give readers joy like that.

60

Lazaro Condo
no one writes a *Wreck*
of the Deutschland
for you so

why does your name still
haunt me
after all this time—
no sainthood

but a column inch
no byline
with your peasants

urging land reform
and finding dirt and a bullet
in a ditch in Chimborazo?

North Sydney 1974

61

A prostitute or mistress turns Madonna, and a toyboy
sporting arrows in his flesh assumes the pose.
He knows the glory hole is busy. He can wait.
Bernini's swooning nun has got what viewers only fake.

They've waited centuries, these saints, to hit the toe,
but they delay a while for us to imitate.
The artists' models are so good at what they do,
behind the scenes, like porn stars whose assistants

stand nearby but out of frame to wipe the sweat,
adjust the lights, hand round the sandwiches and
drinks and change the sheets. Let's keep our minds on higher things.

A glass case on an altar in a chapel on the side
contains a midget, mummified, dressed in a chasuble:
such opulence, such other-worldly love.

When I get tired of being who I am,
I recollect the poet Mitchell in a spotlight in the Globe,
and in the front bar of the Kiwi up in Symonds Street
with his cricket kit straight from a game. A lovely bat.

But that duende couldn't last. At Oriental Bay, years later,
walking westward with my friend Chris Moisa, I went past
a muttering man lost in a world of private Angst.
Chris said, 'My God, that's David Mitchell'. And we stopped.

We were invisible to him. No sign there either of the man
who called a woman the fifth season, of the voice that held a rose
up in the air so clear we saw as well as heard,

a voice that offered silver dreams while it declared
'my name is Yorick, steal away, the worm is in me'.
Voice that stilled a crowded room inside the Globe.

63

Last night I thought how much I'd like to talk
once more with Ken, but he is gone. He would have liked
the *Writer's Chapbook* quip by Ammons, whom he loved—
that forcing poems into being is like going

to the bathroom when you've got no urge to pee.
An *Ars Poetica*. Agreed. No poem wants
to spill the beans. Just let it be. Go clean
the gutters, learn a language, take up sewing.

Take the dog out for a walk. No dog? Get going.
Get a haircut. What, no hair?
Don't hang about. It isn't coming. Get a job,

or read a brochure, book a flight.
Get on that plane. Get out of sight,
and meet the poem where it wanted you to be.

64

In Tarkovsky's *Solaris*, the hero's long-dead wife
is resurrected in his mind and in reality,
repeatedly, no matter how he tries to face the fact
that she was mortal and she died, except

the evidence of breath is so compelling.
How that movie plumbs the pitch of grief,
the *horror vacui* when some dear-loved one dies.
My parents went. Some friends as well.

The world is smaller for their loss
though no day passes without some display of growth
and proof of change: grape into raisin, leaf

to compost that will feed the vine again.
Men fight and kill and add to earth. We live with that.
In spite of which, if you should die—

65

Here I take time out to thank my family
for allowing me to keep my injured cat
who had the road-sense of a turtle, and for all
I know, was certain in his cat-mind that he was one

but much faster on his feet, and though a swimmer,
less inclined to dive for food. But I digress.
The car that hit him took away eight cat-lives
and left one, so he and I turned melancholy.

Can one like a creature so much, though it cannot
talk of Schubert, that you'd call the friendship 'love'?
New York poet Dick Frost told an audience in Wollongong

his cat could not have friends here in Australia to call up
and to chat with. That is true. But when my cat looked up
and said, 'Me out', and 'Prowl', I wondered.

                                        Wollongong 2002

66

John Fields, in the hospice, gives a lesson
in absurdity. He asks me, 'What's the news,
who's doing what to whom, who's winning?'
This is like a bonsai seminar, but serious.

The visiting reporter, come to say farewell,
unravels parish scandals, misdemeanours round the traps,
and John remarks, 'It seems, I've missed out
all the gossip while I got on with my life'.

What's there to say? The war continues,
and the Stock Exchange holds steady on bizarre,
the population of velours has shrunk to zip?

I say we're stories that we tell ourselves
about ourselves—to see if we believe them, then we die,
and others tell more lies about us. Right, he says.

Armidale 2013

67

They think it's sublime. It's endorphins.
They're tigers on heat in a cage.
They'll donate their couplings to science.
They cannot imagine age.

They think love's a green Maserati.
But it comes in a flat-pack, post-paid.
Some parts have gone missing in transit.
It's a two-seater bike. It's beige.

They listen to friends who remarry,
asserting 'I will', 'unto death'.
Meanwhile, onlookers wonder at so much wasted breath.

Every time's like the first time.
A smashing new day begins. This time it's all or nothing.
As usual, the wedding bells ring.

68

'What sort of love poem's that?', you ask—
'The "Look at us in bed" stuff's all been done.
You need a gimmick now to make a splash,
say interspecies sex or maybe hitting on a nun'.

Thanks, reader, for the question from the floor.
It's marvellous how others get their kicks.
Mine, for what it's worth, is states of mind.
Go online if your bag is outré sex.

Percy Grainger liked a whip-around.
Vanessa Duriès found it exciting to be bound.
Anais Nin and her daddy found inventive ways to screw.

Of course, I've read John Wilmot, Porter, Sappho,
Kandel, St Vincent Millay, and Hacker, too,
but reader, tell us all about the things you like to do.

69

Perhaps it happened she was tired of living.
Sex in nightclubs or soon after didn't square
with what she wanted. Who can say what she expected?
She was wrecked. She went to air.

She wore her lips out kissing men and women
who like her were faking lives.
I wondered what she looked for in a lover,
and what any of us think we mean by that—

the fleeting fuck and then goodbye, or link for life.
She was a friend of sorts when she could talk.
Some men and women in her life had names,

and some were silhouettes on speed and ice in disco lights.
The last, a distillation, long expected,
took her home to stay the night.

70

This is not a poem. You are so right. What we want
is some new theory, form, etcetera. I do not like
cliché catalogues of action in the sack. Or being stalked
by ancient talk, that *ferai chanson d'amour* jazz, or

playing parts and planting fantasies in other people's heads,
e.g., as Severin did to Wanda. O puh-lease—not her in furs,
the Cruel Fair!—such superstructure, rhetoric glossing
what pop singers say directly, just like children when they want
                                               a treat or toy.

Who can believe the shonky spiel, the male lead's
'I'm your patient log-man, babe', when what he means
is 'I'm pretending, don't cha know, to be the real deal,

but we know love's for the birds—I've spilled enough of me,
and now, despite the bleeding-heart pop-schlock I'm wearing
on my sleeve, believe the words I say are true'.

71

My sister won't see wattle bloom this year
nor any other. Strange, the thought. The train
emerges from the southbound rain that blears the windows
and the forest lost in fog.

The countries where she made her pilgrimage
are mysteries to me. Now the gulf between us
widens more. Her practice in her clinics,
and her faith were foreign to me in my craft.

There is such beauty that she never saw in places
like these woodlands and soft hills I pass each day.
At length her family took her from her home.

Children thread the saturated paddocks to their college
on the rise. Now there is sky between the trees.
Rain fills the channels, and the wattles are in bloom.

                                        Castlemaine 2015

72

The night I stayed with friends,
I saw their grandchild,
thirteen, was she then? so shaken,
on discovering she had turned into a woman,

that speech left her, not from shyness that
the others or I sat there, but bewildered
at the world that had unmade her,
that had turned her from a child into a woman.

When we finished eating and dispersed to other rooms,
she reappeared along the corridor and sat down
at the piano and played not once but three times,

that sonata movement full of Sturm
and Drang until the house rang, and that instrument,
as if its heart were breaking, beat with her.

Bellingen 2012

73

No man is a hero to his dentist, but the inverse may be true.
Dave Santleben, comedian, this poem is for you.
One look, and 'Stickjaw toffee took no prisoners, I see.
You've got a busted picket fence where others keep their teeth'.

The men who ran the clinics in the suburbs of my youth
were funny as a funeral and as sunny as a Psalm.
A chair-side manner was a growled instruction to be still.
Modern science meant a slow belt-driven dental drill.

An anaesthetic hurt as much as going at it raw.
Who wondered why so many dentists smelt like whisky priests
from putting up with kids who howled and adults who threw fits?

Those men (no women back then) learned their practice in a war.
Then I encountered laughing gas and sympathy and wit.
So, Dave, fangs for the memories, and P.S., the caps still fit.

Armidale 1980

74

They quoted laws that made it right to kill her,
and he bent and with his finger wrote in dust.

The morals police demanded his opinion
while the rubbernecks stood round,

until he straightened up and said, 'Let anyone
who's never sinned be first to throw a stone at her'.

And then he stooped to write again.
The lawyers left, the oldest first and then the rest.

And then he stood and asked the woman,
'Tell me, where are your accusers?' and, 'Has any man

condemned you?', and she answered, 'No one, sir'.
'Then neither do I. Go, and leave your life of sin'.

Who was her lover? What was written
that made clear their law was dust?

75

My parents' God was a moody man who mooched about the house
decked out in kit we'd seen in an uncle's wartime snaps from the
Middle East.
He lived on shelves, in books, and prints on walls, with his dolled-
up hair,
and a 'What's with the sheep on the movie set?' look on his puss.

The eldest of my sisters was a saint without a halo,
and the rest were standard issue, though it didn't seem our God
had any favourites if the hit-rate of rewards for wearing out
our knees in prayer was any guide. The sad-sack ikons stared

back at us when we joked about the heart-shaped lamp
that God wore on his shirt. My Sunday mornings were a torment.
Weary people, huddled under coloured glass and statues, mouthed
responses,

and their features ached from years of holding lookalike expressions.
I remained a pious puppet till the ritual turned to memory,
and the pictures into kitsch, and God three letters on a page.

76

My parents chose to travel via Christ's wounds through the world.
They thought of rich evangelists as egoists and thieves,
and priests who pried on people's private lives as creeps.
Hymns they loved when young had been usurped by feel-good slop.

There was no fake emotion in their lives.
The wonder is they saw the world as good, and so it was.
Black holes appeared as molecules to them, the grain of sand
that William Blake saw, and the mustard seed that Christ held in his hand.

I first encountered physics playing tennis
as the ball leapt from the sand and met the racquet in my hand.
Why it was so, came to my mind, such mind that Hopkins had opined

had mountains, mined till out of sight,
as psilocybin's understood to put the mind in flight.
How could a body that was wounded shed such light?

77

My mother the Surrealist lived in a liminal zone
like the mood of a great bank foyer
or a grand hotel's palm court where former lovers meet
and find each other noble: mythic space,

from which she said an owl and a cat in a boat
had declared, to the sound of small guitar,
their love and espousal.
Where did she learn feline speech?

She told me how a band of beast musicians
went to Bremen, and a cat had gone to London
to investigate a Queen, and how a small boy had been

counselled by the cat that seemed to turn up
in each story, that if he turned back, he'd thrive. I checked.
He did. So what was there I could not love about her?

Armidale 1998

Afterword

Never a prize-gathering writer, I snavel Wordsworth's description of his poems to label mine 'my shame in crowds, my solitary pride'. Nic Holland's grandly titled 2008 DVD, *Poetry in Motion: The works and life of Michael Sharkey*, sported Les Murray's embarrassing blurb rating me 'the most neglected of our major poets'. I read this as facetiousness, believing that if, as Byron said, 'poets are such liars and take all colours like the hands of dyers', it takes one to know one. At any rate, I agree with Murray's view that poetry should be outwardly, and upwardly directed, though I do not write AMDG, as Catholic schoolboys used to do at the top of each page (a dead giveaway to secular markers of State exams).

In the late 1960s, my co-worker and novelist friend Gus O'Donnell showed sixty or so of my early sonnets to his friends at South Head Press. The *Poetry Australia* editor, physician Dr Grace Perry, wrote to me that I would get over the condition, and told me, 'Get modern'. I ditched Petrarch and the Elizabethans, and read Lowell, cummings, Hardy (the 'Travel' sonnets), Waldman, Hacker, Berryman, Berrigan, Frost, and others. Somewhere back then, I read in *Chinese Literature* magazine that the sonnet form had travelled the silk road to the west and fetched up in Andalusia and Provence. The translated Chinese examples read like ordinary talk in English. So before I moved to New Zealand for some years at the end of the sixties, I accordingly burned all but a handful of souvenirs of my early drafts.

In New Zealand, I sent newer work to *Landfall*, *Islands*, and other journals in New Zealand and Australia and beyond. I read James Baxter's *Jerusalem Sonnets* and *Autumn Testament*, as everyone did. His influence was palpable. By the time I returned to Australia and met Les Murray, he told me he'd thought of me as a New Zealander. If only.

This present gathering survives my cull from 300 or so poems concerning aspects of love, written over almost sixty years. Mostly undated poems were written on unsorted scraps, and I shuffled the whole into some syncopated order that reflects the stochastic work of memory. I see no reason why the poems should conform to Renaissance patterns—

the fault of my discarded earlier series. The quasi-formalism of the stanza structure that I have adopted stems from my reading of the vernacular sonnets of Giuseppe Gioacchino Belli and Bertolt Brecht. In its favour is plasticity that embraces dramatic monologue, dialogue, epigram, and meditation on the comedy of transience and survival.

Michael Sharkey
March 2023.

www.ingramcontent.com/pod-product-compliance
Lightning Source LLC
Chambersburg PA
CBHW031003090426

42737CB00008B/663

*9 7 8 1 9 2 2 5 7 1 9 0 8 *